WETLANDS

John Willis

LET'S READ
AV2
BY WEIGL™
ADDED VALUE • AUDIO VISUAL

www.av2books.com

Go to www.av2books.com, and enter this book's unique code.

BOOK CODE

F737848

AV² by Weigl brings you media enhanced books that support active learning.

AV² provides enriched content that supplements and complements this book. Weigl's AV² books strive to create inspired learning and engage young minds in a total learning experience.

Your AV² Media Enhanced books come alive with...

 Audio
Listen to sections of the book read aloud.

 Video
Watch informative video clips.

 Embedded Weblinks
Gain additional information for research.

 Try This!
Complete activities and hands-on experiments.

 Key Words
Study vocabulary, and complete a matching word activity.

 Quizzes
Test your knowledge.

 Slide Show
View images and captions, and prepare a presentation.

... and much, much more!

Published by AV² by Weigl
350 5th Avenue, 59th Floor New York, NY 10118
Website: www.av2books.com

Library of Congress Control Number: 2015956189

ISBN 978-1-4896-4181-6 (hardcover)
ISBN 978-1-4896-4182-3 (softcover)
ISBN 978-1-4896-4183-0 (single-user eBook)
ISBN 978-1-4896-4184-7 (multi-user eBook)

Printed in the United States of America in Brainerd, Minnesota
1 2 3 4 5 6 7 8 9 0 19 18 17 16 15

112015
111315

Project Coordinator: Jared Siemens
Design: Mandy Christiansen

The publisher acknowledges Corbis Images, Minden Pictures, Shutterstock, and iStock as the primary image suppliers for this title.

WETLANDS

Contents

This is a wetland.
A wetland is a place where the ground
is covered with shallow water.

Wetlands can be found in most places on Earth. Some are wet all year. Others are wet only some of the time.

South America has the largest natural wetland on Earth.

Wetlands are like large sponges. They store water from rain and melted snow.

Moss is a plant found in wetlands. It can hold large amounts of water.

Caracara birds keep capybaras healthy by eating bugs in their fur.

Venus flytraps get their food from insects instead of the soil.

Frogs hide in duckweed to stay safe.

A wetland ecosystem is a place made up of animals and plants that need each other in order to live.

Algae make air for salamanders growing in eggs.

Beavers make new wetlands when they build dams.

Plants are an important part of a wetland ecosystem. They provide food and shelter for the animals that live there.

Mangrove trees are shelter for families of fish.

Cattail roots are food for muskrats.

Water lily seeds are food for many wetland birds.

The hollow trunks of cypress trees are often home to wood ducks.

Rice plants are food for marsh rice rats.

Mudskippers are fish that live mostly on land.

The great blue heron uses its sharp bill to hunt for food in the water.

A crocodile can hold its breath underwater for up to two hours.

Many different animals make their homes in wetlands.

Muskrats are covered in waterproof fur.

Bog turtles spend winter underwater in deep mud.

Plants and bacteria remove waste from wetlands water. Removing waste from water makes it clean.

Wetlands make water safe for people to drink.

People drain water from wetlands to make room for buildings and farms. Draining wetlands hurts the animals and plants that live there.

More than half of Earth's wetlands have been lost since 1900.

The United States has laws that keep its wetlands safe. People must replace any wetland that they destroy.

Today, the United States has more than 1,000 manmade wetlands.

Wetland Quiz

See what you have learned
about wetland ecosystems.

Find these wetland animals
and plants in the book.
What are their names?

KEY WORDS

Research has shown that as much as 65 percent of all written material published in English is made up of 300 words. These 300 words cannot be taught using pictures or learned by sounding them out. They must be recognized by sight. This book contains 69 common sight words to help young readers improve their reading fluency and comprehension. This book also teaches young readers several important content words, such as proper nouns. These words are paired with pictures to aid in learning and improve understanding.

Page	Sight Words First Appearance
4	a, is, place, the, this, water, where, with
7	all, are, be, can, Earth, found, has, in, most, of, on, only, others, some, time, year
8	and, from, it, large, like, plant, they
10	by, food, get, keep, their, to
11	air, animals, each, for, live, made, make, need, new, that, up, when
12	an, important, part, there, trees
13	home, many, often
14	its, land, two, uses
15	different
16	people
19	been, have, more, than
20	any, must

Page	Content Words First Appearance
4	ground, wetland
7	South America
8	moss, rain, snow, sponges
10	birds, bugs, capybaras, duckweed, flytraps, frogs, fur, insects, soil
11	algae, beavers, dams, ecosystem, eggs, salamanders
12	fish, muskrats, rats, roots
13	ducks, seeds, trunks
14	bill, crocodile, heron, mudskippers, underwater
15	mud, turtles, winter
16	bacteria, waste
19	buildings, farms
20	laws, United States

Check out www.av2books.com for activities, videos, audio clips, and more!

1 Go to www.av2books.com.

2 Enter book code. F737848

3 Fuel your imagination online!

www.av2books.com